LEARN WITH MOONBIRD

weather

Illustrated by Mike Higgs

Written by Sally McNulty

© Mike Higgs 1984

ISBN 0 00 197064 X

Printed in Italy

Collins

London and Glasgow

When Moonbird watches Earth from his home on the moon, he can see the weather all over the world. Moonbird and his friend Pug were planning to visit Earth. Their friend Sarah was having a birthday party.

The moon friends were looking for a clear space to touch down. The atmosphere over the Earth was very cloudy. Winds were blowing the clouds.

The *atmosphere* around Earth is very important. It holds the air we breathe. It warms the Earth by trapping the sun's rays like a blanket. Weather is made in the atmosphere. The weather we have today may come from a place far away, blown to us by wind.

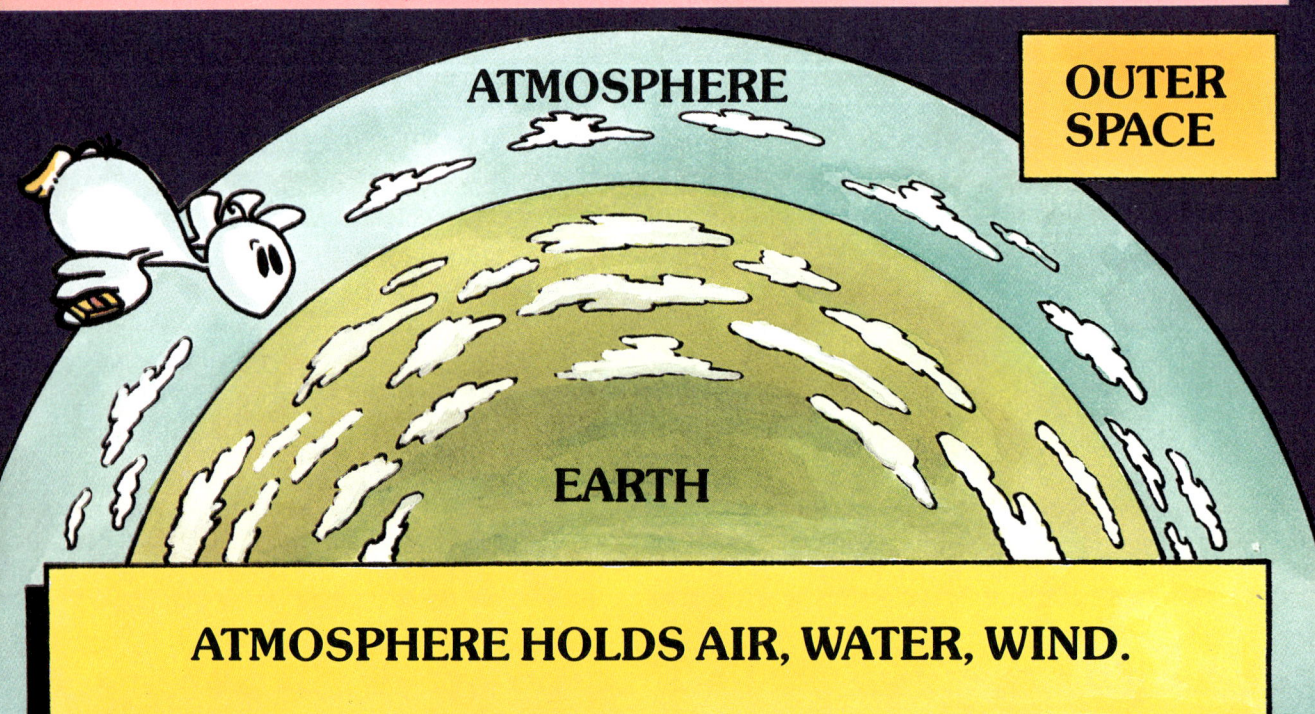

ATMOSPHERE

OUTER SPACE

EARTH

ATMOSPHERE HOLDS AIR, WATER, WIND.

"What are clouds made of?" asked Pug.

"Clouds are made of millions of tiny droplets of water called water vapour," said Moonbird. "Warm air holds more water vapour than cold air. When warm wet air meets cold air, some of the vapour turns back into water. This is *condensation*."

CONDENSATION

MOISTURE IN AIR

TURNS TO

WATER

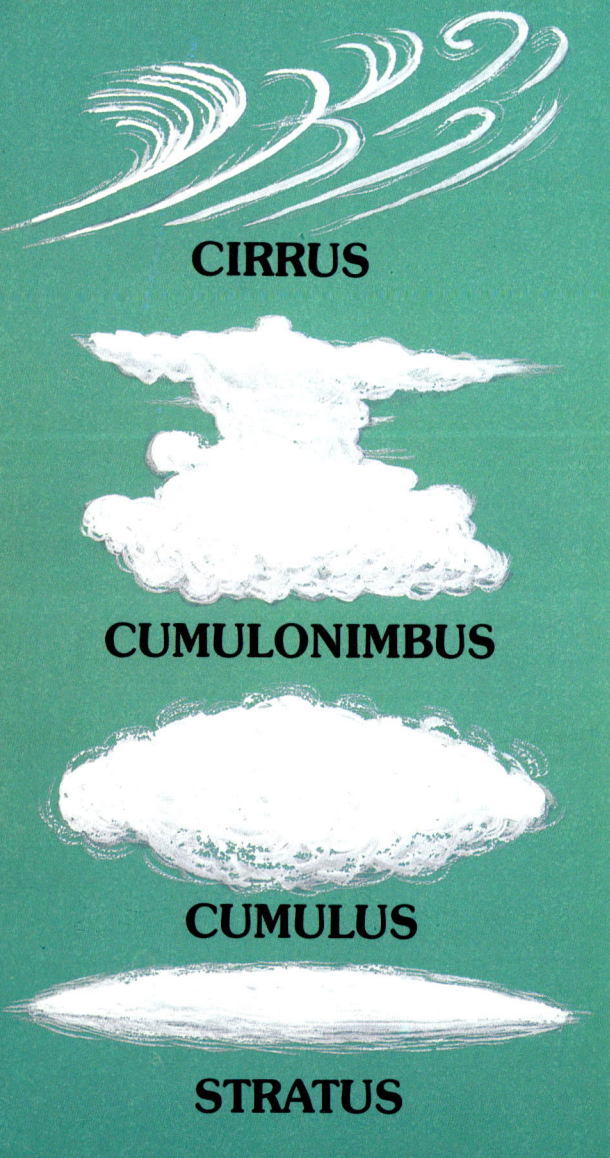

CIRRUS

CUMULONIMBUS

CUMULUS

STRATUS

"How is rain made, Moonbird?" Pug asked.

The sun's warmth pulls up water vapour from the oceans, lakes and rivers," said Moonbird. "It even pulls vapour out of the ground. This is *evaporation*. As water is heated by the sun it slowly disappears. When the vapour meets cold air it condenses back into water to form clouds. The drops in the clouds become big and heavy. They become so heavy they fall back to Earth as rain."

EVAPORATION: WATER BECOMES VAPOUR IN AIR. VAPOUR CONDENSES TO FORM RAIN CLOUDS.

"What about snow and hail?" asked Pug.

"The air high above the Earth is very cold," said Moonbird. "When rain clouds move up to this colder air, water in the clouds freezes to tiny crystals of ice. The ice joins together to make snowflakes."

SNOWFLAKES HAVE SIX SIDES.

EVERY FLAKE IS DIFFERENT.

"Hail forms when a raindrop is thrown up and down by the wind in a thundercloud. As it goes up it freezes. As it comes down it picks up a layer of water. This goes on until the drop turns into a little ball of ice."

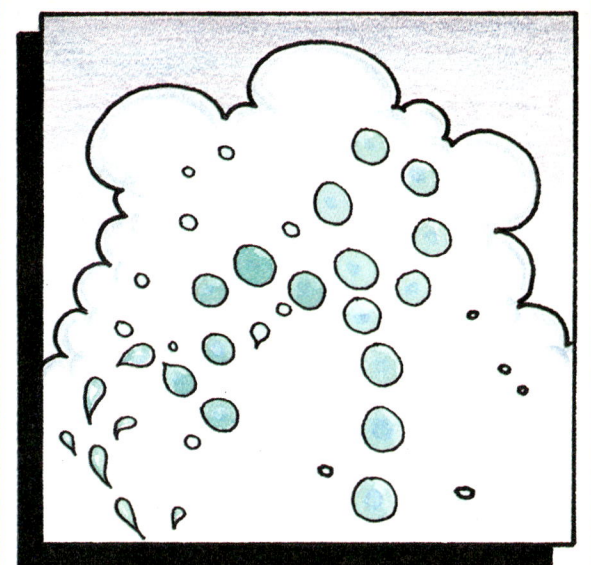

SNOW AND HAIL MELT BACK INTO WATER.

"Have you ever seen dew or frost?" Moonbird asked Pug. Pug shook his head, no. "Dew forms when warm air touches cold ground. As the air cools tiny drops of water collect on plants and grass. If the weather is cold enough, the dew freezes and turns to frost."

DEW

FROST

"Another kind of condensation is fog. Fog is a large cloud that lies close to the ground. It is made of tiny drops of water. Mist is a thin fog. When the sun warms the air, the fog and mist disappear through evaporation."

FOG

MIST

"Earth's air is always moving," said Moonbird. "Heat from the sun warms the land. Warm air over the land begins to rise. It moves up into the sky to become a large current of air. Then cooler air moves in to take its place. The moving air current is wind."

"Wind blows over many different kinds of land and water. The land and water can be hot or cold. The air can be wet or dry. These differences can change the weather from place to place."

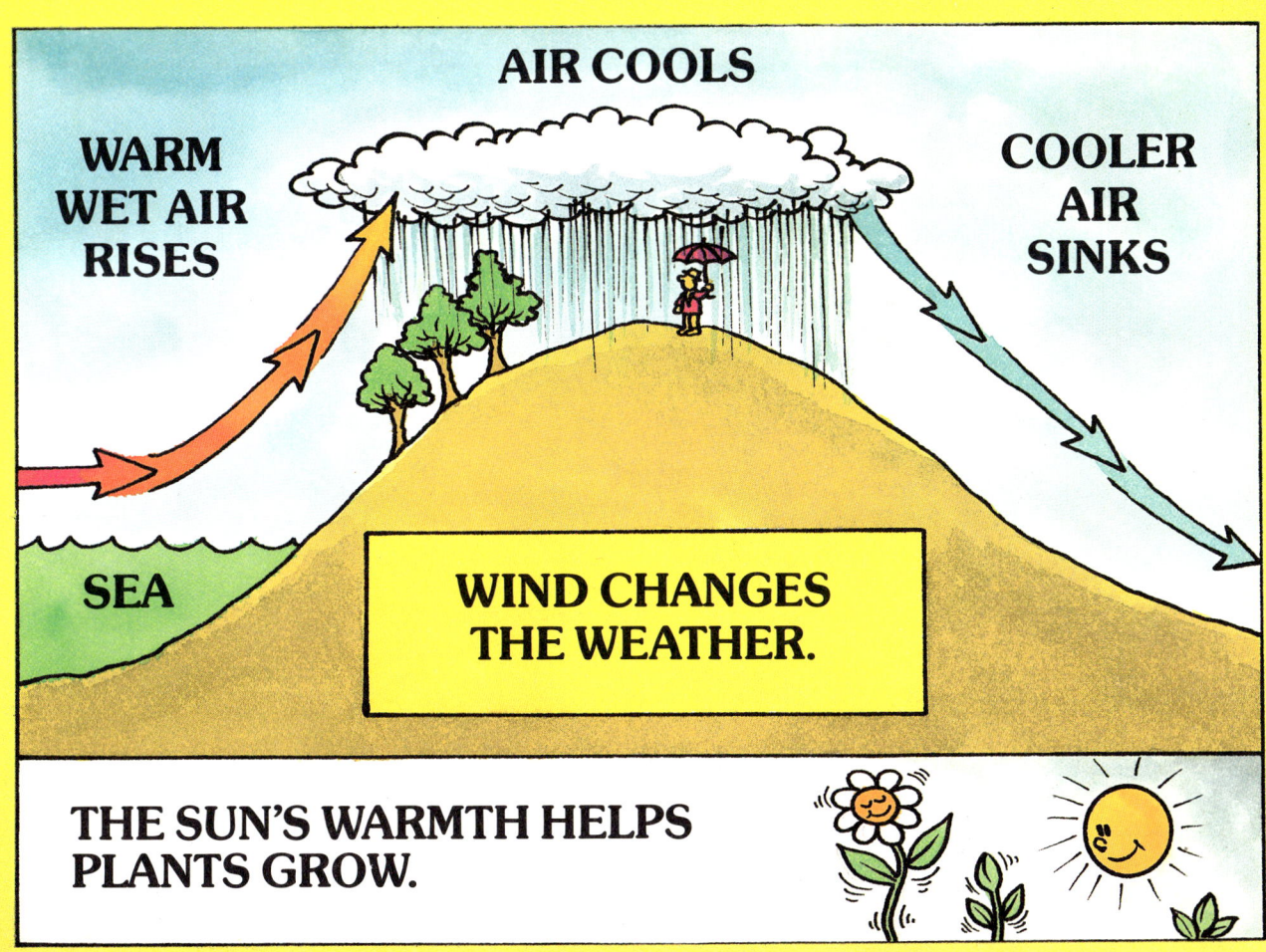

AIR COOLS

WARM WET AIR RISES

COOLER AIR SINKS

SEA

WIND CHANGES THE WEATHER.

THE SUN'S WARMTH HELPS PLANTS GROW.

COLD AIR

WARM AIR

"If wind comes from the North or South Pole, it will bring cold air. If the wind comes from the Equator, the air will be very warm. When wind blows across oceans, it draws water vapour out of the sea and brings us wet

MOIST AIR

HOT DRY AIR

weather. If wind blows across a desert, it brings hot dry air. These different winds are so big they are called air masses. An air mass is many miles high and wide."

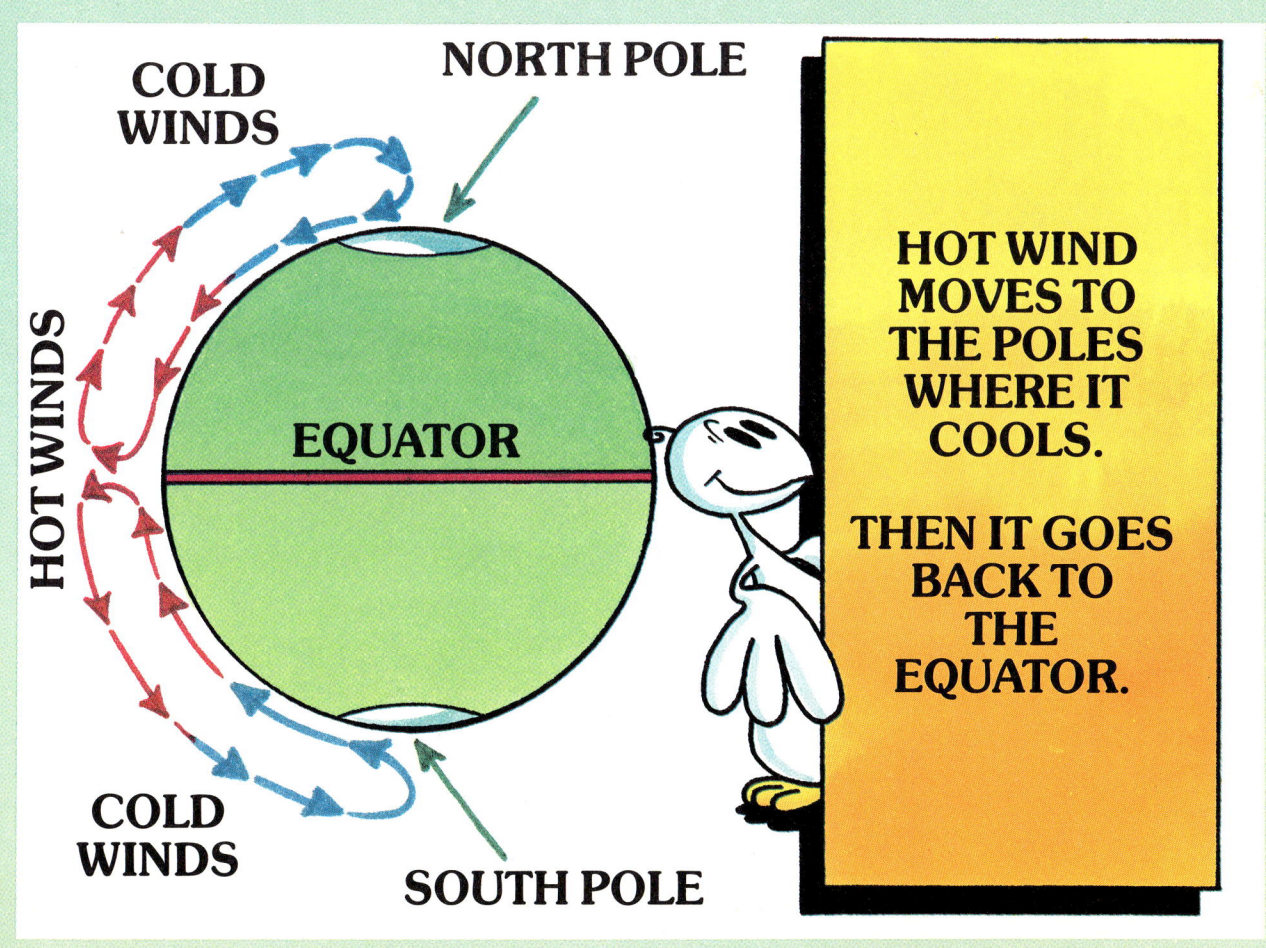

COLD WINDS

NORTH POLE

HOT WINDS

EQUATOR

COLD WINDS

SOUTH POLE

HOT WIND MOVES TO THE POLES WHERE IT COOLS.

THEN IT GOES BACK TO THE EQUATOR.

"I think I see a way through the clouds now," said Moonbird. The friends rode a moonbeam quickly to Earth.

"Oh dear," said Moonbird. "We are still a few miles away from Sarah's house. I hope we make it in time for her party."

"I think we have arrived in the middle of a cold front," said Moonbird. "Just look at that rain!"

"What is a front?" asked Pug.

RAIN WATER FEEDS PLANTS AND FLOWERS.

"I can explain," said Moonbird. "When a warm air mass and a cold air mass come together, they form a front. If the warm air mass is stronger, we get warmer weather. If the cold air mass is stronger, our weather turns colder. Inside a front warm air is rising

and cold air is falling. As the two kinds of air mix together clouds form from the water vapour in the warm air. The clouds rise until they reach very cool air. Then they drop rain. Wherever air masses meet as a front there is rain."

COLD FRONT

WARM AIR

COLD AIR PUSHES
UNDER WARM AIR

RAIN

"Two powerful air masses are coming together right now," said Moonbird. "Big winds are blowing the trees."

"They are making me cold," said Pug.

"The weather is turning into a storm," said Moonbird. "We'd better take cover."

STORMS HAVE STRONG WINDS AND HEAVY RAIN.

"What's that, Moonbird?" asked Pug pointing to the sky.

"That's lightning, Pug," answered Moonbird. "It happens when static electricity grows inside a cloud. As it gets stronger it becomes an electric charge. The giant spark of electricity you see is called lightning."

"The electric charge is so strong that the air around it explodes and makes the noise we call thunder. Lightning is always drawn towards tall things such as tall houses and trees. Never stand under a tree in a storm."

LIGHTNING IS AN ELECTRIC CHARGE.

Pug was shaking from the wet and cold. "Things could not get any worse than they are right now," he grumbled. "We are never going to get to Sarah's party on time."

"Things could get a lot worse," replied Moonbird. "I see something bad coming. Help! It's a tornado!"

Just then a mole poked his head out of a hole in the ground. "Quick. Jump in here for safety," he said.

COLD
AIR

COLD
AIR

WARM AIR

"A tornado is a column
of spinning air,"
explained Moonbird.
"It reaches from the
ground to the clouds. It is born over land
when a mass of cold air blows over a mass of
warm air. The warm air wants to go up. The
cold air wants to go down. The masses push
hard against each other. Then the hot air
finds a way through the cold air and shoots
up through it making a powerful wind that
spins. As the winds move they suck up
anything in their path—even houses and
trees."

"Is a hurricane the same thing?" asked Pug. He was feeling safe inside the mole hole.

"No," said Moonbird. "A hurricane is a giant storm born over warm seas where the air is hot and wet. Air circles around as it rises. It spins faster and faster. The wind howls and the rain beats down for hundreds of miles around."

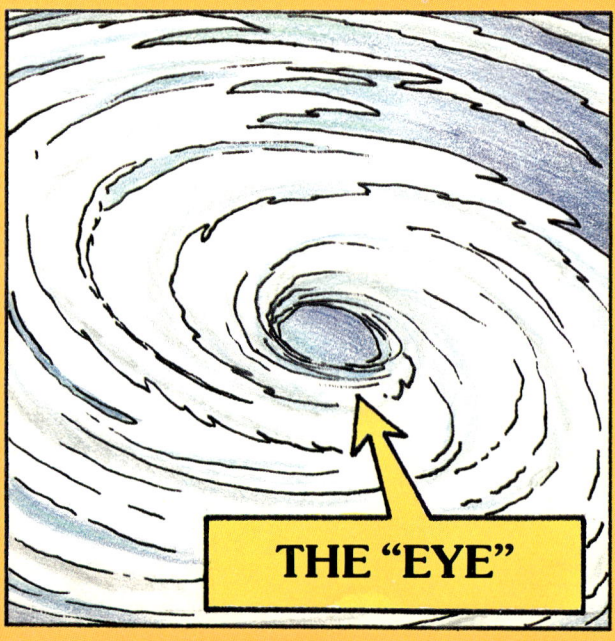

THE "EYE"

"The centre of a hurricane is calm. It is called the "eye" of the storm. The storm clouds can reach up into the air for 8 miles. Hurricanes travel from the sea to the land. Their winds can tear the roofs off houses. They can uproot trees and carry them for miles in the air, dropping them far away."

HURRICANES HAVE MANY NAMES:

**CYCLONES
TYPHOONS
WILLY WILLIES
BAGUIOS
TROVADOS
PAPAGAYOS**

Pug poked his head out of the hole. "The tornado is over and so is the storm," he said happily. "We might make it to Sarah's house after all." The two friends thanked the mole for saving them and continued on their way.

"Look Moonbird," cried Pug. "The sun is coming out. Look at the beautiful rainbow!"

WHAT MAKES A RAINBOW? THE SUN SHINES INTO RAINDROPS IN THE AIR. RAINDROPS REFLECT THE LIGHT, BREAKING IT UP INTO MANY COLOURS.

HAVE YOU EVER SEEN A RAINBOW THROUGH A GARDEN HOSE OR SPRINKLER? OR A FOUNTAIN IN A PARK? YOU HAVE A BETTER CHANCE IF YOU STAND WITH THE SUN BEHIND YOUR BACK.

Sarah was so happy to see her two moon friends. "You're just in time for the birthday cake," she said.

"We're sorry to be late," said Moonbird. "We had a little trouble getting here."

"You can say that again," said Pug.

 Sarah opened Moonbird's present. It was a book about the four seasons. This is what Sarah saw.

THE FOUR SEASONS

SPRING

SUMMER

MARCH

APRIL

MAY

JUNE

JULY

AUGUST

AUTUMN

WINTER

SEPTEMBER
OCTOBER
NOVEMBER

DECEMBER
JANUARY
FEBRUARY